AF265732

DA7Y STORY

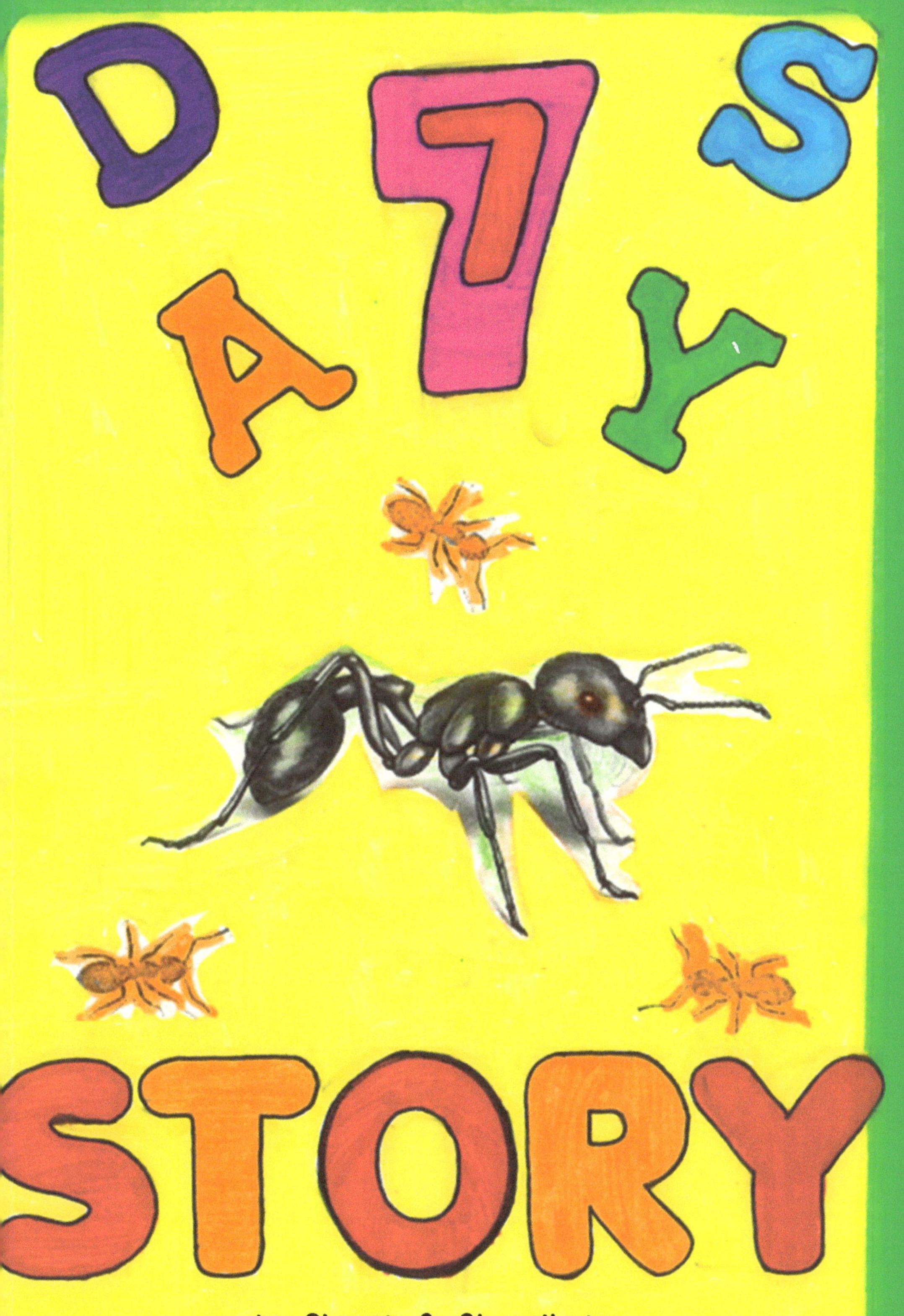

by Shiper A. Choudhury

Illustrated by Sasha Choudhury

WORKBOOK PRESS LLC
187 E Warm Springs Rd,
Suite B285, Las Vegas, NV 89119, USA

Website: https://workbookpress.com/
Hotline: 1-888-818-4856
Email: admin@workbookpress.com

Ordering Information:
Quantity sales. Special discounts are available on quantity purchases by corporations, associations, and others.
For details, contact the publisher at the address above.

Library of Congress Control Number:
ISBN-13:   978-1-957618-78-4 (Paperback Version)
               978-1-957618-79-1 (Digital Version)

REV. DATE: 02/24/2022

DEDICATION

To the reader of this book, to the wonderful children of all ages. Like what I've mentioned before, I wrote many children books. I would like to encourage you all to make your child read more and more. Reading is fun. Reading is the foundation of your feet, our body weight is on our feet without, we are limited from our life. Many things we will miss.

Nothing is wrong with reading. The more you read, the more knowledge your children will be gaining. Read any book, take your child to the library on your free time. Let your child gain experience. Let them explore many, many books in library shelves. Many books are written by historians. Although they are no longer alive and only things that are left behind are the history of written words that make sense to everyone.

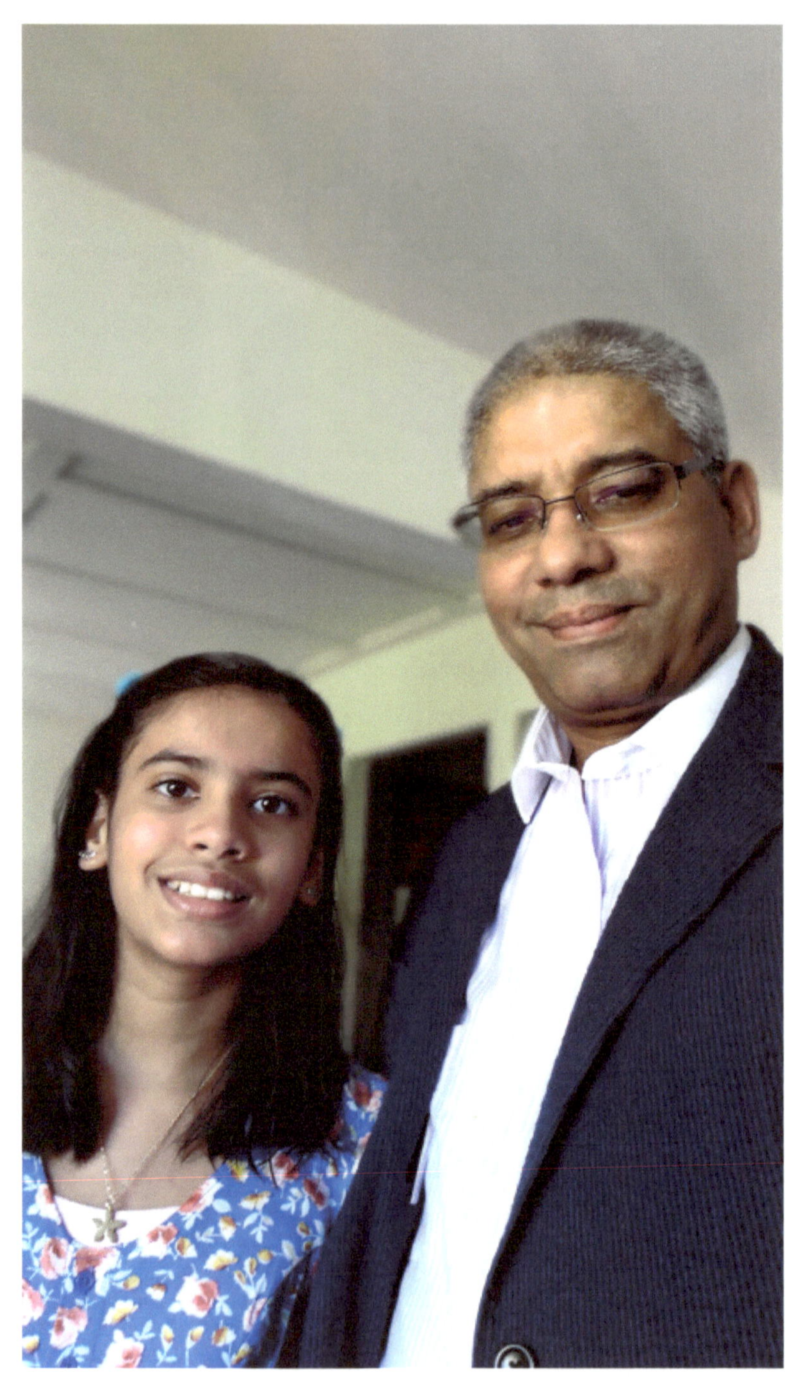

Me and my daughter Sasha

INTRODUCTION

Reading is navigation of life. Reading is map of the highway. You must know how to read in order to survive. Reading is a tool of technology and technology is life created from reading. This is for us to know how read and write and gate is open for your life.

I hope you enjoy reading this short story of ants that me and my daughter have written.

Thank you!!

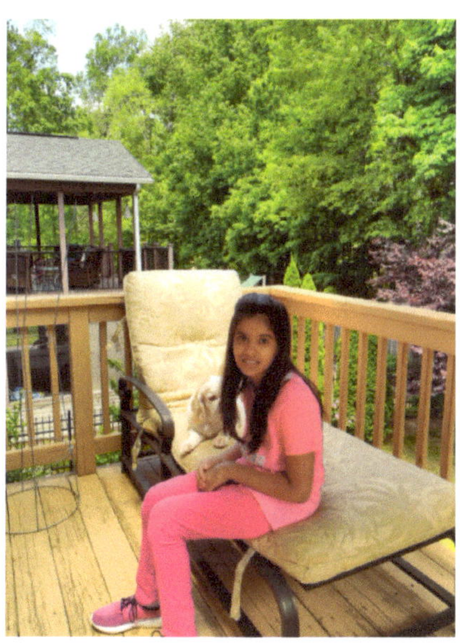

My daughter Sasha, the one who illustrated this book

It is about "Seven Days Ants Story". Me and my daughter went to the public library. We spent couple of hours in the library. For half an hour, we come out for a snack.

We go sit down in one spot then ten to fifteen minutes, we go down, we see a lot of ants that lines up. They are very busy running all around, up and down, across many coming up and many are going down. Busy working like regular business day.

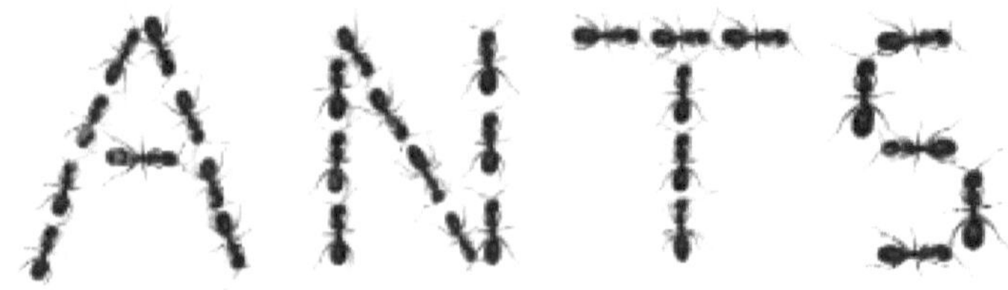

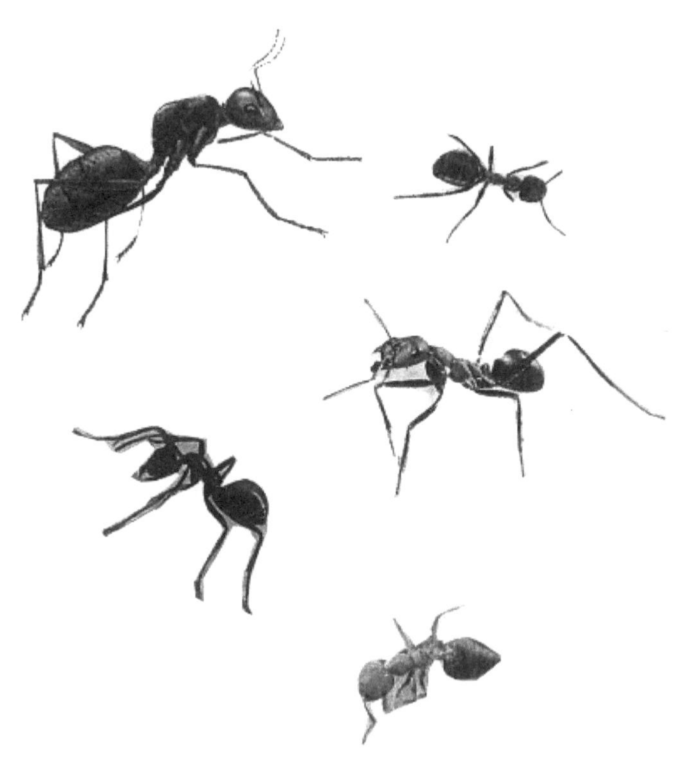

Beautiful it is summer, very nice blue sky, no rain, no dry crispy day. We are having snacks and chatting looking down talking about ants and all the ants. One night, near where we are sitting down, it is very interesting to look at them.

Ants are moving very fast, it is like they are on the clock or whatever they are doing, the ants have to meet the deadline running against time.

They are very friendly, my daughter was asking me, "Can I take one of them on my hand, see what they do?", I said, '"I am not sure about it, if ants bite or not? I can tell you it is safe because since it is not red color, then it is okay. I know because Red ones, they seem very friendly and they walk very slowly but they bite even it is little bite, it can become red and start to itch after while it goes away". That was my experience from one bite.

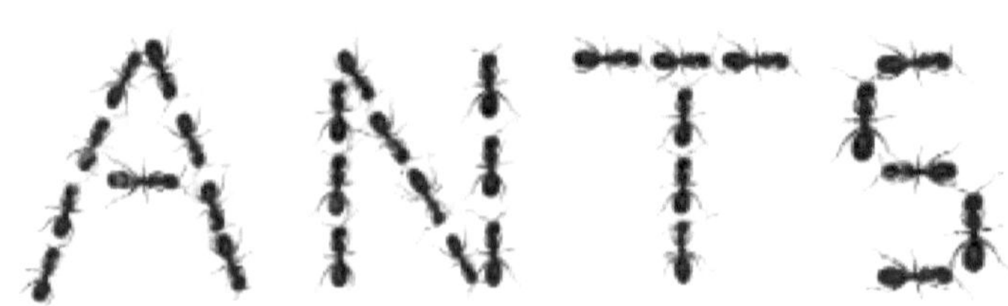

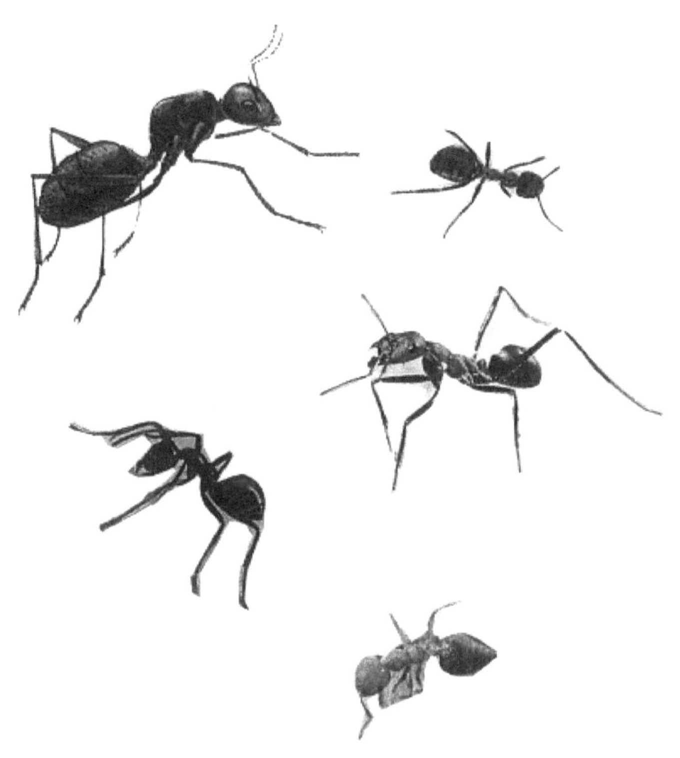

Today is Tuesday afternoon. Weather is sunnier and gorgeous day. Wind is very calm and very relaxing. We headed to the library to spend few hours. Before we come out in some spots where we spend half an hour or more, my daughter asked me, that from the library to the sitting spot. "You think all the ants are still there?", I said, "Well, let's go and find out what our beautiful ants are up today".

When we went to our spot, just like Monday, it seems to us that it is same on Tuesday, busy running around up and down, crisscross, left and right like a flea market. We have noticed almost same amount of ants, more or less. They are not bothering anyone; they are just busy on whatever they are doing. I just reminded my daughter to just don't step on them and be careful where she steps because if she steps on them accidentally, whole of them can die.

We don't want that to happen. They are very peaceful not harming anyone. We finish our snacks, I said to her, "Let's go back inside the library for half an hour or so".

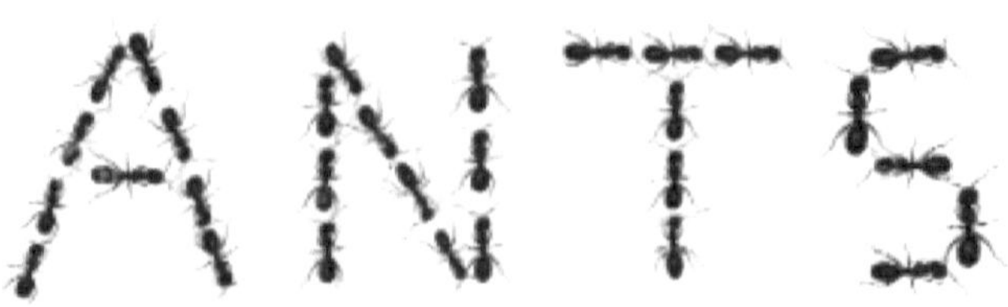

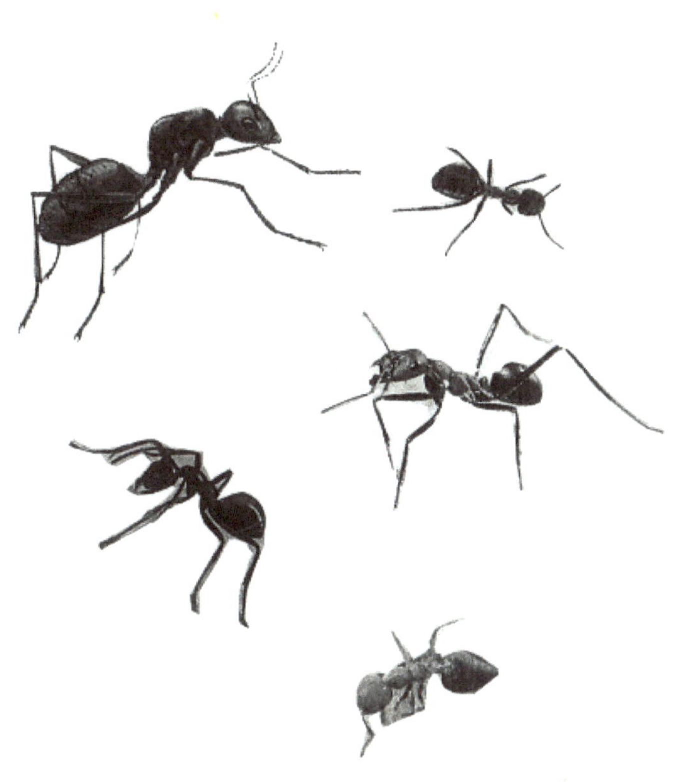

We will come back again tomorrow and is Wednesday, another day. We can visit them if the ants are there again. So, it is Wednesday, weather is bright hot and sunny blue clouds moving above us so peaceful and calm when we look in the sky. We headed back to the library for two hours straight.

When we come back out again, we went back to our spot where we sit. Guess what, no changes just the way we left on Tuesday afternoon. It is same on Wednesday, tireless and running around up and down and very happy without any conflict among them just like the blue sky above all of us. The clouds moving flawlessly so does the ants moving up and down fearlessly. We finish our sandwich and say bye to the ants. "See you guys tomorrow, hope it doesn't rain at night. If it rains they will be washed away. We will miss them and never see again.

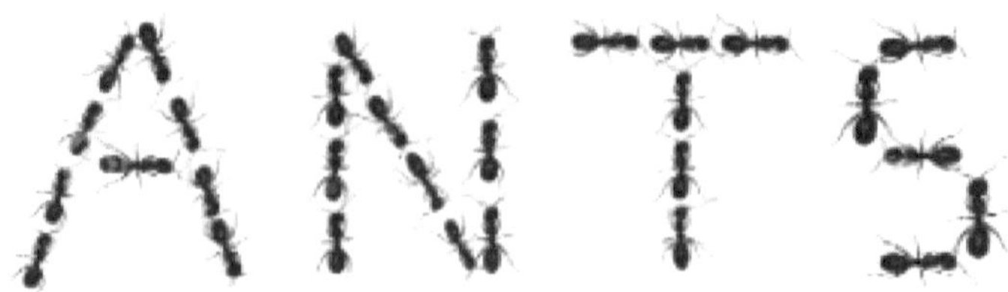

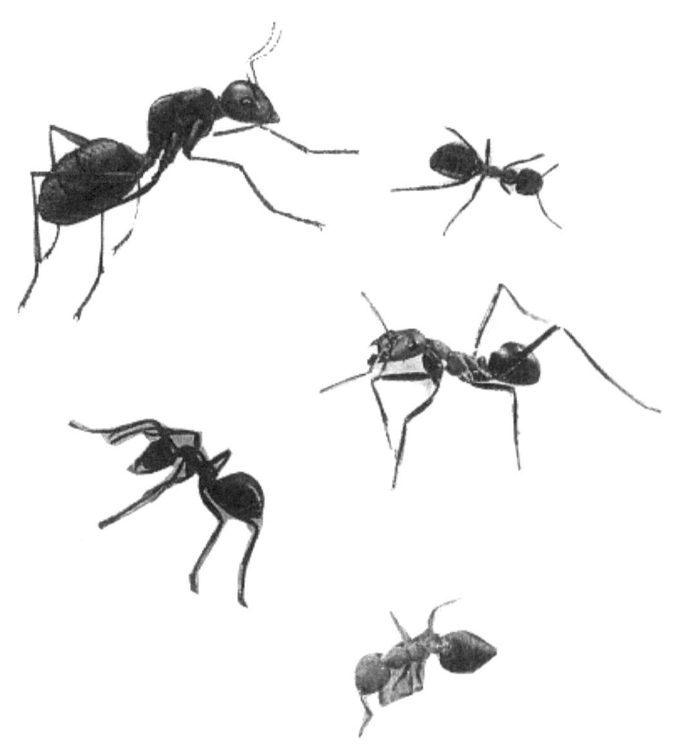

Well, another crispy bright sunny Thursday afternoon. We headed to the library and we look out for few books. We read few pages here and few pages. Then after we spent an hour or so, we went to the store across the street from library and buy cold drinks and snack. We walked back to our original spot where we sit and eat out our snack.

Guess what, we are surprised and very shocked. My daughter said that today is Thursday. I said to my daughter, "Yes, today is Thursday". But I also said, "Wait, we came down here Monday, Tuesday, Wednesday and we are here today, which is Thursday.

Did you notice there is no change? All these days, they are right here within 2 feet of space. They are extremely busy going up and down without harming anyone. Busy with their own business.

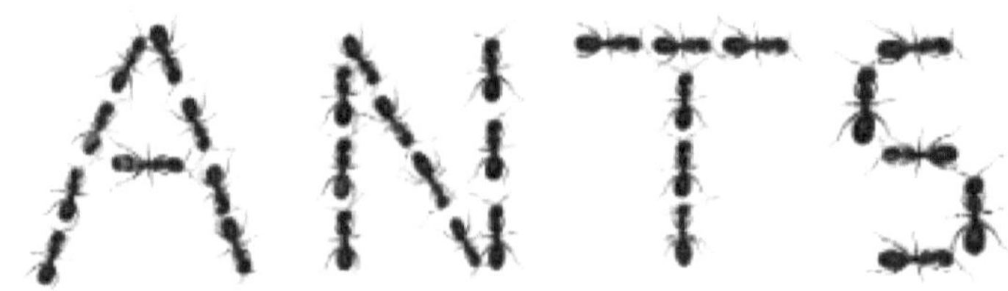

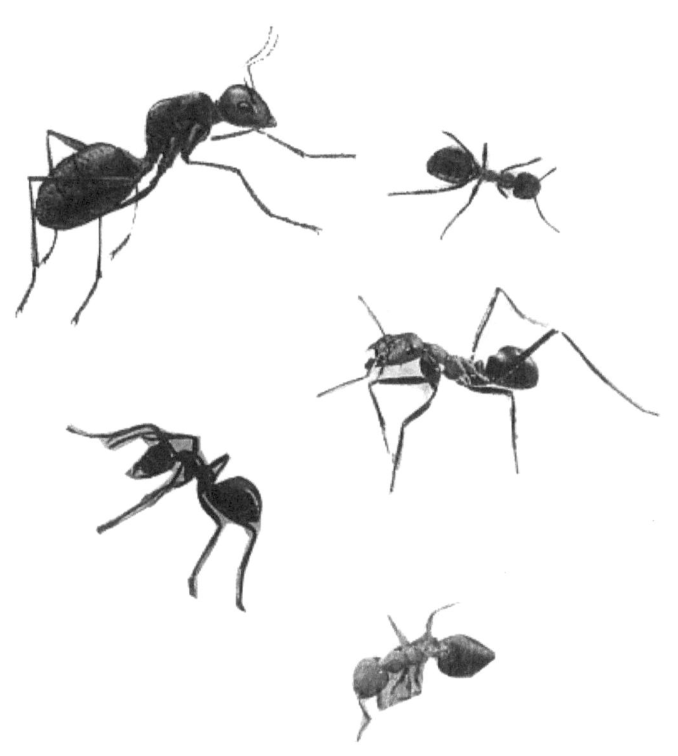

I was telling my daughter that there might be thousands of them under the ground. They might have a travel plan to go up and down the tunnel.

So they will not have stampede and don't crush into each other. So that they can have safe journey through the tunnel.

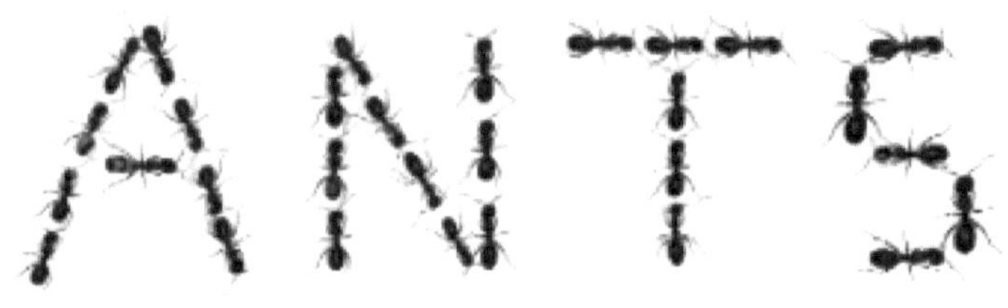

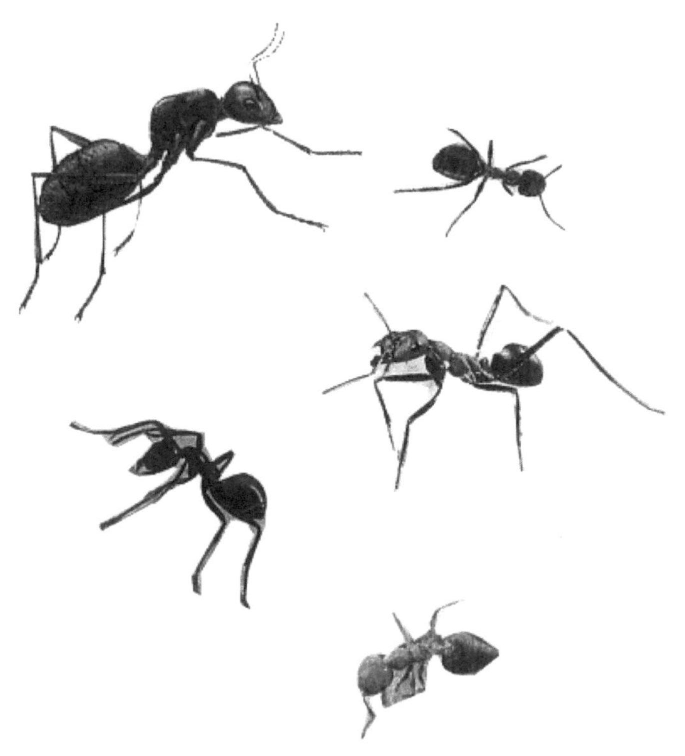

Well now, Thursday is finished. So far, we have visited and went to our usual spot. Now that is Monday, Tuesday, Wednesday and Thursday went by that added up four days.

We left on Thursday afternoon and hope that it will not rain tonight or every ant will be washed away by the water. Rain can be unpredicted at any time.

We usually go to the library around first or second week of the month. Seven days straight for few hours per day. Every day is different day and have some fun with ants while we take a short break.

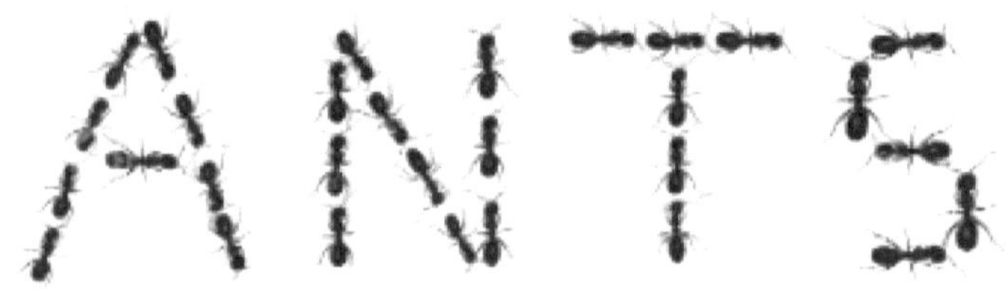

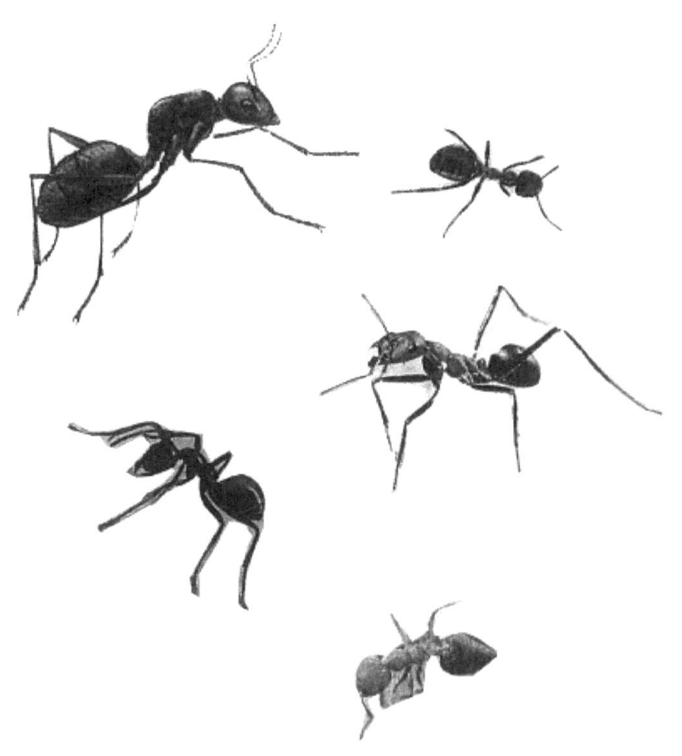

I told my daughter, "Well, today is what day, can you tell me? ", she answered, "It is the fifth day, we are going to the library". Do you think that ants took the day off? I asked her. The question since they worked so hard every day. She answered, "They should take one day off since they are working so hard.

When we went to our regular snack break spot, guess, what a surprise? There is no change, no sweat and they are busy as usual and having fun without any fear in them. No bumping to each other, walking criss cross, up and down, very calmly and very respectfully.

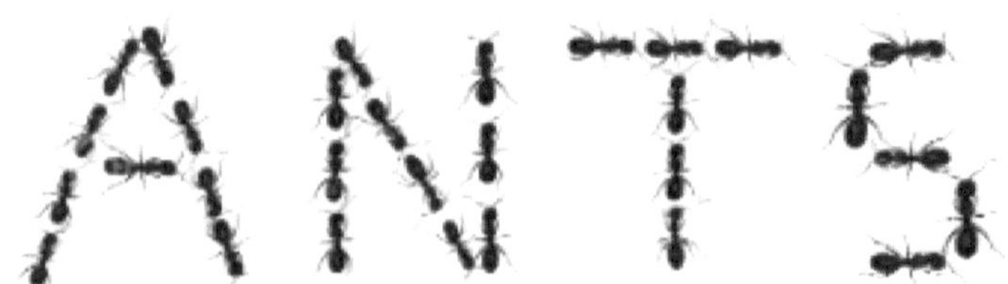

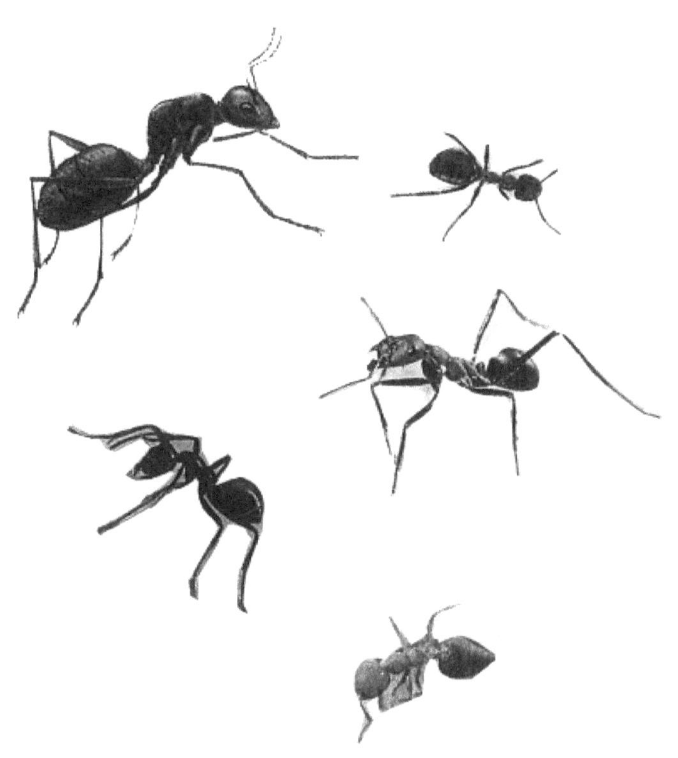

Week is almost finished and we did go to the library, five days already. Let's count the days we went. Monday, Tuesday, Wednesday, Thursday and today is Friday.

That's make us five days. This five days, all ants within their boundary are walking. Now, since today is Saturday and yesterday was Friday. Today, the library is closed early we will skip snack and have lunch straight. But before we leave like to go to our spot, we hang around for few minutes like ten minutes a day is just so beautiful.

Our ants, we called them friendly since we see them so many times already.

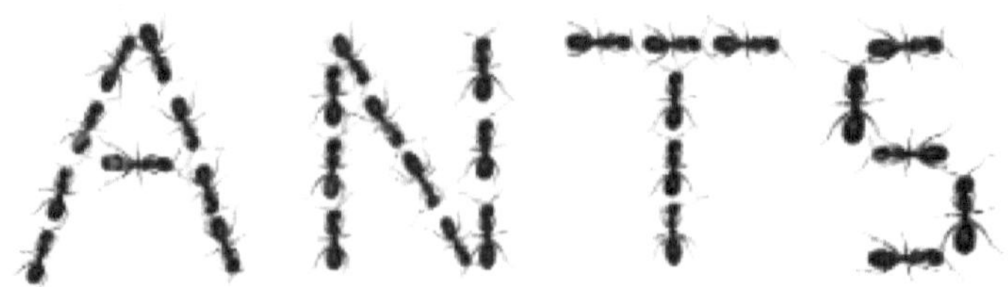

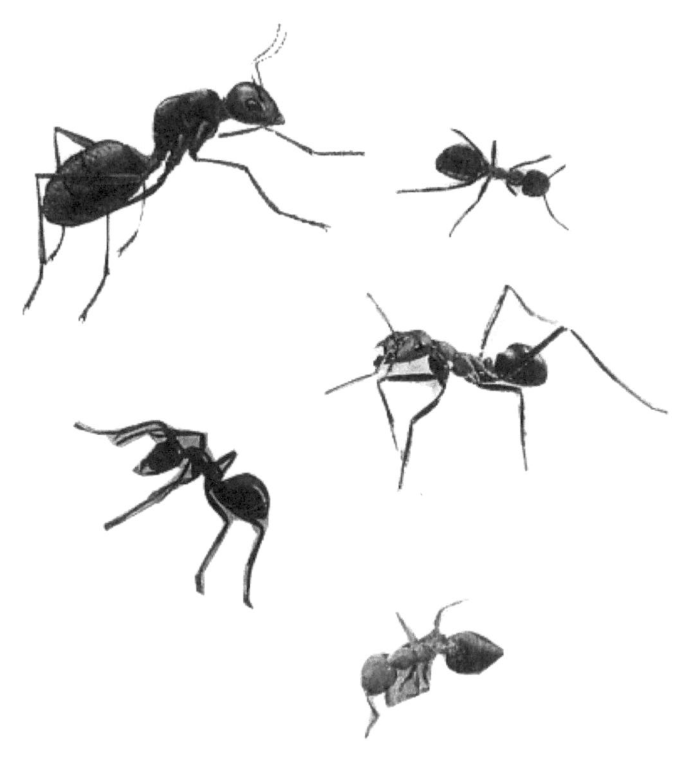

Today will be the sixth day out of seven days, what a surprise. All the ants are enjoying the sunny Saturday afternoon as usual like all other days.

No stress, no harm, no fear, no tiredness and no laziness. Strong as they can be.

We told them we will leave you guys now enjoy the day, maybe you all should rest one day. You know tomorrow is Sunday should take a day off. But we will be here at library for short time then we will go for a walk out to the store then we will eat something.

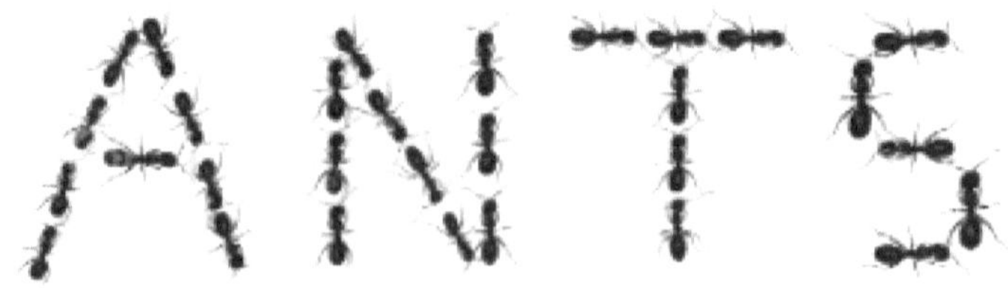

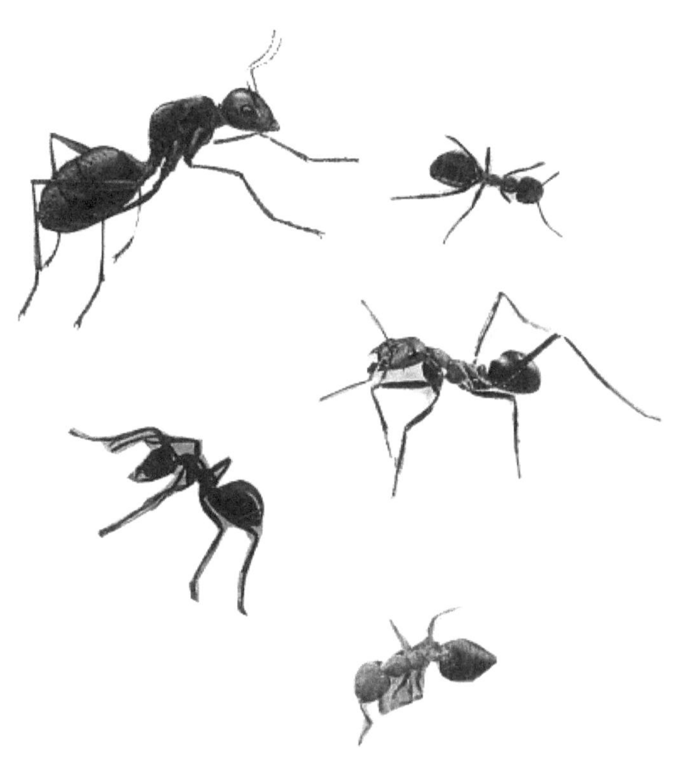

Well, well, what a surprise. Guess what again today is the seventh day and today is Sunday. Let's count the days again. Start with Day 1 -Monday, Day 2- Tuesday, Day 3 - Wednesday, Day 4-Thursday, Day 5- Friday, Day 6- Saturday and the last day of the week Day 7- Sunday.

What a wonderful seven days we had.

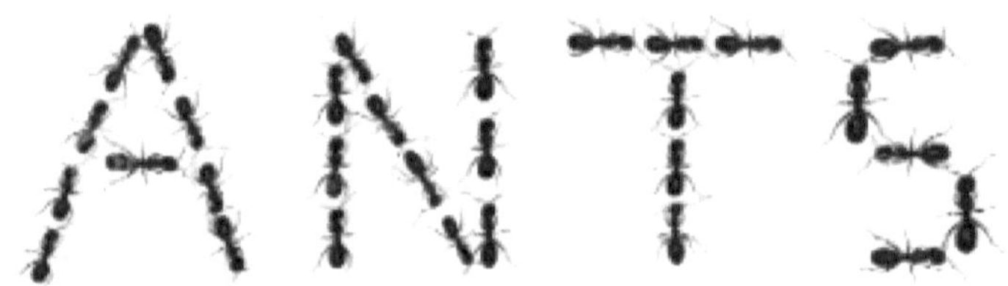

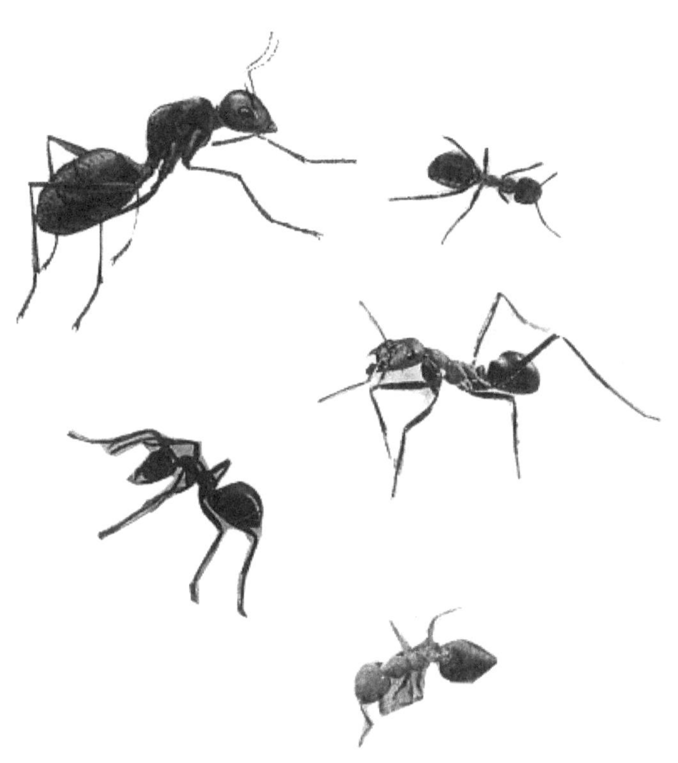

Library is closed early today. Everyone needs some rest from work. Spend some time with family and friends. We also spent little time not too long, before we left.

We just want to make sure one last time before we go and to see where they are going. We are very surprised at first we thought we are in the right place, I asked my daughter, "Are we in the correct place where we eat our snack?".

She said, " Yes, this is the spot where there are ants". And I am a little confused because they are not here out all today. She said there are all here, take a close look. I told her, she did and she said nothing is here. No ants at all.

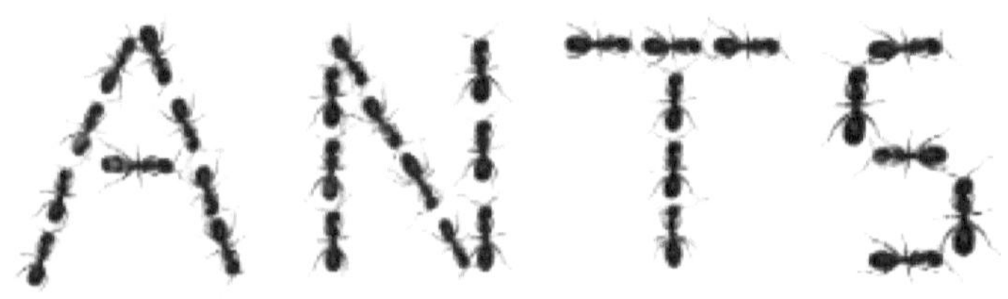

I said, told you but are we in the right spot?

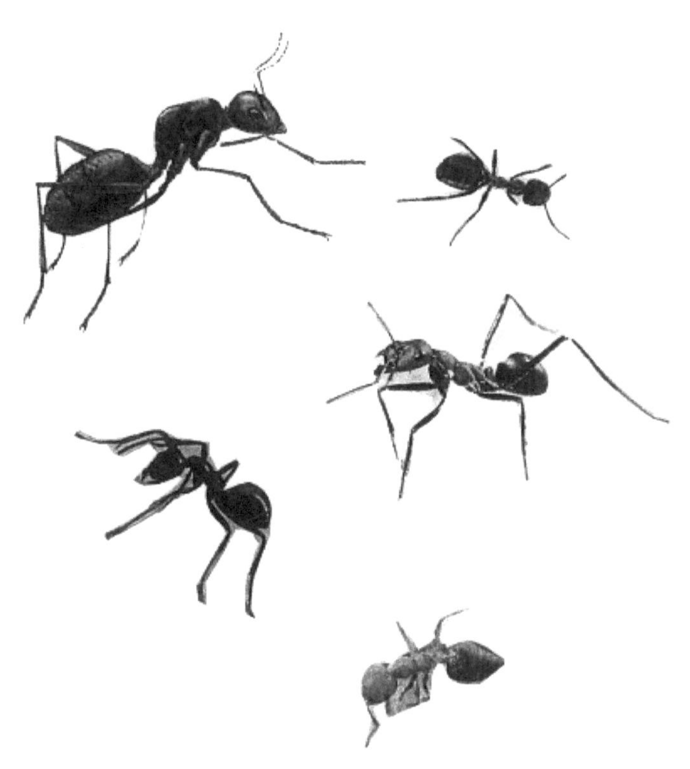

Now she is asking me the same question I asked earlier. We both got shocked of what happened to them. It didn't rain and the weather is beautiful Sunny. We looked on each other and we are very surprised and said that today is the seventh day. So we named our book " 7 Days Ant Story".

Don't forget today is Sunday. They took a day off so they can sleep, rest a little, relax and have some fun meet with friends and family.

When I told her that, she laughed and laughed. So meet with friends and family. The ants I said to her yes the ants. I started to laugh and laugh too with my daughter.

Finally, we went to our way and ended up in a restaurant to eat. We got hungry maybe from laughing.

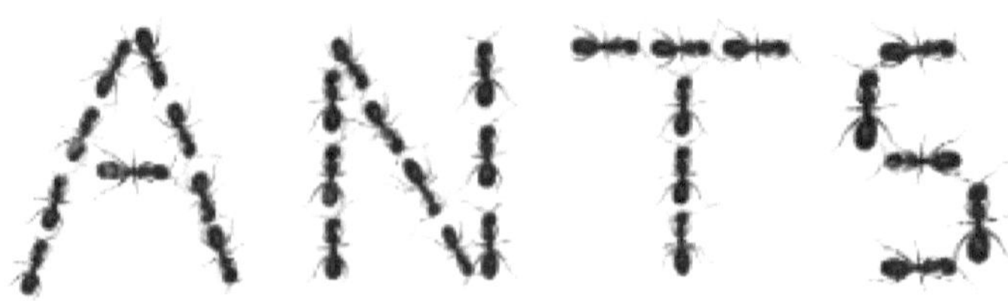

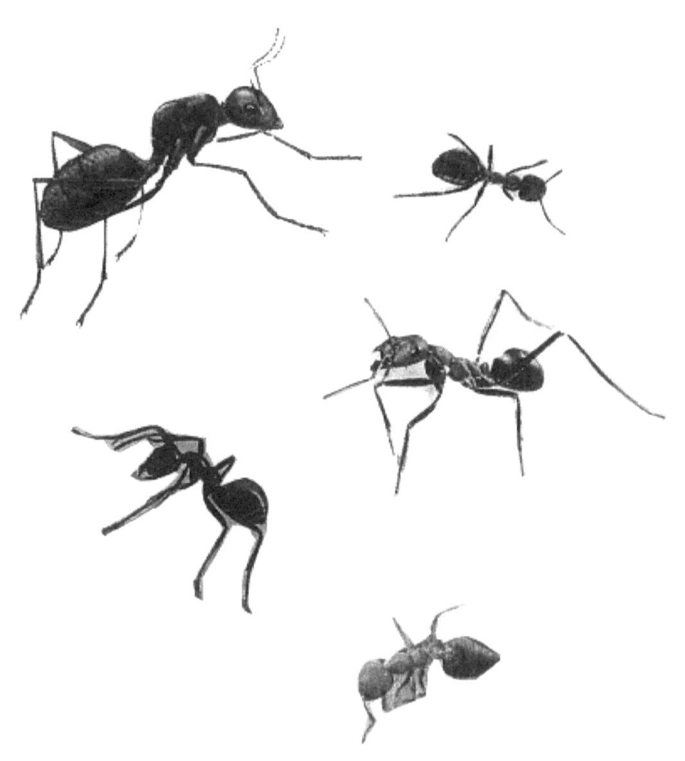

QUESTION:

Do you think ants sleep at night?

If you can, you can do your own investigation!

THE END

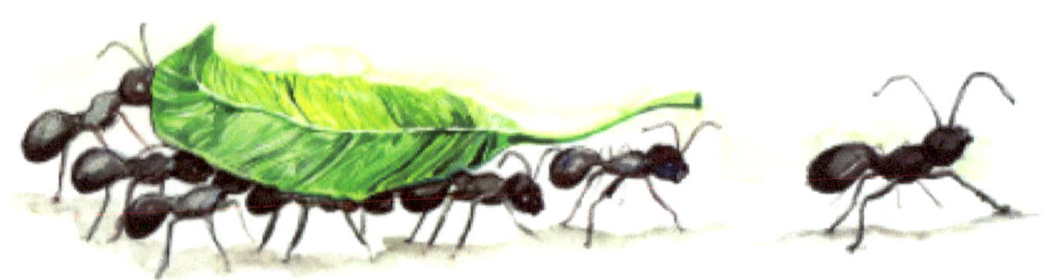